Financial Literacy Basics:

Buying a Car & Understanding Auto Insurance

Financial Literacy Basics:

Buying a Car & Understanding Auto Insurance

2020/21 Edition

GREY HOUSE PUBLISHING

https://greyhouse.weissratings.com

Grey House Publishing
4919 Route 22, PO Box 56
Amenia, NY 12501-0056
(800) 562-2139

Weiss Ratings
4400 Northcorp Parkway
Palm Beach Gardens, FL 33410
(561) 627-3300

Independent. Unbiased. Accurate. Trusted.

Published by Grey House Publishing, Inc., located at 4919 Route 22, Amenia, NY 12501; telephone 518-789-8700. Grey House Publishing neither guarantees the accuracy of the data contained herein nor assumes any responsibility for errors, omissions or discrepancies. Grey House Publishing accepts no payment for listing; inclusion in the publication of any organization, agency, institution, publication, service or individual does not imply endorsement of the publisher.

2020/21 Edition
ISBN: 978-1-64265-585-8

Table of Contents

About This Guide

Welcome!

Grey House Publishing and Weiss Ratings are proud to announce the fourth edition of *Financial Literacy Basics*. Each volume in this series provides readers with easy-to-understand guidance on how to manage their finances. Designed for those who are just starting out, as well as those who may need help handling their finances, volumes in this series outline, step-by-step, how to make the most of your money, which pitfalls to avoid, what to watch out for, and the necessary tools to make sure you are fully equipped to manage your finances.

Each of these eight volumes focus on specific ways to take the guesswork out of financial planning—how to stick to a budget, how to manage debt, how to buy a car or rent an apartment, how to calculate the cost of college, and how to start saving for retirement—all information necessary to get started on your financial future. Each volume is devoted to a specific topic. Combined, they provide you with a full range of helpful information on how to best manage your money. Individual volumes are:

- How to **Make and Stick to a Budget**
- How to **Manage Debt**
- Starting a **401(k)**
- Understanding **Health Insurance** Plans
- **Renting an Apartment** & Understanding **Renters Insurance**
- Calculating the **Cost of College** & Understanding **Student Loans**
- **Buying a Car** & Understanding **Auto Insurance**
- What to Know About **Checking Accounts**

Filled with valuable information that includes helpful, hands-on worksheets and planners, these volumes are designed to point you toward a solid financial future with clear suggestions, supportive guidance and easy-to-follow dos and don'ts.

About This Guide

Unless your city has a good public transportation system, owning a car is probably essential to your ability to work, play, and generally enjoy a modern lifestyle. And along with car ownership comes the need to purchase automobile insurance. In fact, very few people factor the cost of auto insurance into their decision about which car to buy. What most people don't realize, however, is that it is often very easy to save hundreds of dollars per year on auto insurance by simply educating yourself and shopping around.

This is where Weiss Ratings can help. This publication is designed to give you a good overview of your auto insurance options. It walks you through the considerations for selecting the appropriate type of insurance and coverage levels, plus it gives you instruction on how to find the best price from a strong, reputable insurer.

Best of all, you can rest assured that the information presented here is completely independent and free of bias. Weiss Ratings does not sell insurance, we are not connected with any insurance companies, and we won't make a single penny should you decide to purchase a policy from one of the companies listed in this guide. Our goal is to simply help you make the best decision possible - for you.

Financial Literacy Basics: Buying a Car & Understanding Auto Insurance

Part 1: Buying a Car

For many, having reliable transportation is a necessity. Unless you live in a city with convenient public transportation, you're going to need a car to get to work, run errands, and get from place to place.

Buying a car is a major purchase, so make sure to explore all of your options, and do your research, before you make your final decision.

Buying New, Buying Used & Leasing

If you're in the market for a new car, you generally have three options:

Buying a New Car – this is the most expensive option, but it is long-term. A new car is under warranty for the first few years, if something needs to be replaced, and new cars are generally very reliable and can be driven for 10 years or more.

Buying a Used Car – this is often considered the best value for car shoppers, since it's far less expensive to purchase a used car than a new one. Most newer model used cars will last for many years, so you can expect to drive it for a while before it needs to be replaced. But, you want to make sure that you're getting a reliable car that won't end up costing you at the repair shop.

Leasing a New Car – this option lets you drive a new car at a much-reduced price. This might seem like a good idea, but when the lease is up, you have no car and no equity. Beware of lease mileage restrictions. Most leases set a maximum amount of miles that you can drive the car during your lease. If you go over this number, you pay an extra fee for every extra mile you have driven. Pay close attention to additional fees and potential charges for things like scratches and dents.

You'll want to be aware of some important information before you start car shopping.

Know Your Budget

Knowing how much you can afford for your car is an important first step. Make a simple budget by writing down what you earn in a month, and all of your expenses. This will allow you to figure out how much you can afford to spend on a car. You'll need to budget for a 10% down payment, your monthly car payment, car insurance, gasoline and routine maintenance.

There is more information on making a budget in another guide in this series, *Financial Literacy Basics: How to Make a Budget and Stick to it.*

Know Your Credit Score

Unless you plan on paying for your car in cash, you will need to secure financing for your car. Checking your credit report and knowing your credit score when you are considering financing or leasing a car will help you decide how much of a loan you can manage.

You can get a free copy of your credit report every 12 months. To order your credit report, visit www.AnnualCreditReport.com, or call 1-877-322-8228.

Find Out What Car is Right for You and Your Budget

There are hundreds of cars, trucks, SUVs and minivans to choose from. The answers to these questions will help you narrow down what car is right for you.

1. **How many people will you be driving around?** This is one of the most important factors when deciding between a smaller car and an SUV or a minivan.

2. **How much cargo will you be hauling around?** If you need lots of room for sports equipment, a minivan or an SUV might be a good pick. If you need to haul heavy loads or equipment, a truck is the way to go.

3. **Is fuel economy important to you?** The type of engine and transmission in your car will determine your fuel efficiency. A smaller four-

cylinder engine provides better fuel efficiency, but lacks the power of a six-cylinder engine. Electric cars and hybrids (an electric car that can also run on gas) have excellent fuel economy. Diesel engines offer good fuel economy too. If power and handling are more important than fuel economy, you might consider a car or truck with a six- or eight-cylinder engine. If you have a long commute, you will save quite a bit of money over the long term with a car that has better fuel economy.

4. **How important is safety?** You can compare safety ratings on various cars by visiting the Insurance Institute for Highway Safety (iihs.org) and the National Highway Traffic Safety Administration (safercar.gov) websites.

Doing some research on the internet can help you determine what car is right for you. You can read reviews, find out about different options, check safety ratings, the cost of maintenance and insurance, and view photographs, to help you narrow down your list.

Some of the most common sites to help you choose the right car for your budget and needs are:

- Edmunds.com
- Consumer Reports
- Kelley Blue Book

Once you have three top picks, it's time to start shopping.

Financing

If you plan to pay for your car in cash, then you won't need financing, but make sure you have enough cash on hand for taxes and insurance too. Because buying a car is a big purchase, most people take out a loan, or finance, their purchase. It's a good idea to get pre-approved for your car loan before you start shopping for your car.

Usually, your bank or credit union is the best place to start looking for an auto loan. You will most likely get a lower interest rate from your bank or credit union, compared to financing through a car dealership. Make sure you get a copy of the quote from the car dealership in writing, so that you can compare financing quotes from other financial institutions.

When you arrange for financing, there are three main factors to consider:

- **The loan amount.** This is the amount that you will borrow. You can reduce this amount by making a 10% to 20% down payment, which will save you money over the long term.

- **The annual percentage rate (APR).** This is the interest rate you will pay over the course of your loan.

- **The loan term.** This is the number of months that it will take to pay off your loan.

You monthly loan payment will be determined based on these factors. While it might seem like a good idea to go with a longer loan term, which will reduce your monthly payments, keep in mind that this will increase what you pay in interest over the course of your loan.

In the chart below, the lower monthly payment results in an extra $600 over the life of the 5-year loan (vs. 4-year).

By shopping around to find the best rates, you will save money over the long term.

Comparing a 4-Year Term and a 5-Year Term

Term	4 Years – 48 months	5 Years – 60 Months
Purchase Price	$34,000	$34,000
Taxes, Title and Required Fees	$2,200	$2,200
Down Payment (20%)	$7,240	$7,240
Amount Financed	$28,960	$28,960
Contract Rate (APR)	4.00%	4.00%
Finance Charge	$2,480	$3,080
Monthly Payment Amount	$655	$534
Total of Payments	$31,440	$32,040

Source: https://www.consumer.ftc.gov/articles/0056-financing-or-leasing-car#Get

Quote Comparison Worksheet

	Creditor 1	Creditor 2	Creditor 3
Negotiated Price of Car	$	$	$
Down Payment	$	$	$
Trade-In Allowance (If trading in your car, this may involve negative equity)	$	$	$
Extended Service Contract (Optional)*	$	$	$
Credit Insurance (Optional)*	$	$	$
Guaranteed Auto Protection (Optional)*	$	$	$
Other Optional* Products	$	$	$
Amount Financed	$	$	$
Annual Percentage Rate (APR)	%	%	%
Finance Charge	$	$	$
Length of Contract in Months	$	$	$
Number of Payments	$	$	$
Monthly Payment Amount	$	$	$

* Note: You are not required to buy items that are optional. If you do not want these items, tell the dealer and do not sign for them. Be sure they are not included in the monthly payments or elsewhere on a contract that you sign.

Source: https://www.consumer.ftc.gov/articles/0056-financing-or-leasing-car#Get

Locate Cars Through Local Media or Online

Now that you've done your homework and found out which type of car you're interested in, it's time to start looking for your actual car. It's easier than ever now, since you can quickly and easily search through online classifieds. Most car dealerships display the cars they have on sale online too, so it's easy to search through their inventory.

Some of the most common websites to view cars for sale are:

- Autolist.com
- AutoTempest.com
- AutoTrader.com
- CarFax.com
- CarGurus.com
- Cars.com
- CarsDirect.com
- CarMax.com
- Carvana.com
- KBB.com (Kelley Blue Book)
- Tred.com
- TrueCar.com
- Vroom.com

Compare Prices

As you are looking at cars online, keep track of the price of each car you're interested in. The price for a car will vary based on several factors, including:

- **Year, make and model.** This is the year the car was produced, the type of car, and its model, or "trim level." The trim level identifies the standard features included with the car.

- **Options.** These are extra features installed when the car was built.

- **Mileage.** This is the amount of miles the car has been driven. The standard mileage driven per year is 12,000 miles. So, a three-year-old car with 24,000 miles, which is considered low, would be priced higher than the same three-year-old car with 50,000 miles.

Look up the Kelley Blue Book value by year, make, and model at KBB.com to determine the recommended price for the car you are interested in, to see if you are getting a fair deal or not.

Buying a Car Online

Buying a used car online is becoming increasingly popular. Websites like Carvana, Vroom, and CarMax allow you to buy a used car online from start to finish. If you don't want to haggle face to face with a salesperson, buying online is an option. Most sites will deliver the car to you and let you drive a certain amount of miles as a "test-drive" before you commit to purchasing the car.

Check Insurance Rates

Call your insurance company and ask what the rate will be for the cars you are looking at, and factor that cost into your budget. In 2020, the least expensive cars to insure were the Mazda CX-3 Sport, Honda CR-V LX and the Wrangler Sport X.

Keep shopping around until you feel comfortable that you have found a good deal on a car that makes sense for your lifestyle and your budget.

Buying a Car from a Private Seller

If you're buying a car from a private seller, don't be afraid to ask the seller some questions, including why they're selling the car, how long they've owned the car, who has been driving it, how many previous owners it's had, if the car has been in any serious accidents, and its maintenance record. Don't be shy about asking to see the service records, since a car that is well maintained will most likely last longer. If you're seriously considering buying the car, you can purchase a vehicle history report to make sure the car has not been in a major accident. See page 10 for more information.

Shopping for Cars on Craigslist

Craigslist, a popular online marketplace, gives private sellers and dealerships the opportunity to list cars for sale. It can be a quick and easy way to shop for used cars in your area, but you'll want to take extra precautions to keep yourself safe and avoid scams.

If you're considering buying a used car on Craigslist, keep the following in mind.

- If you're not comfortable with buying a car from a private seller, you can limit your search results to dealers only.

- Before going to take a look at the car, call the seller and ask questions. You can get a better sense of the seller with a phone call compared to an email or text message exchange. If you're not getting straight answers from the seller, it might be a good idea to move on. Relevant questions include: ask for additional pictures. Ask if any warning lights appear on the dashboard. Ask if the seller can provide copies of any service records. Has the car had any repairs done recently? How many owners has the car had?

- If the car is in drivable condition, ask the seller to bring the car to a public location, like a busy shopping area, a service station or your local police station so you can inspect it.

- Before making a purchase, have the car inspected by a reputable auto repair shop or a dealership. Don't use a repair shop that is selected by the seller.

- Make sure the seller can produce a clean title for the car.

- When you're ready to buy, ask the seller to meet you at your bank to do the transaction. It's safer to meet in a public space instead of at the seller's location. If the transaction is more than a few thousand dollars, ask the seller if they will accept a certified check from your bank.

- Make sure you have all the necessary paperwork in hand before you pay for the car. The seller will need to give you the car's title. Sign a bill of sale.

- Above all else, make decisions that don't risk your personal safety and with careful thought. Don't be hasty, ask a lot of questions and take precautions to avoid scams.

Be Safe

If you are buying a car from a private seller, take some safety precautions before taking a test drive with a stranger in the car.

Ask the seller to show you a photo ID, and take a picture of it. Email or text that picture to a friend or family member, just to be safe.

If you don't have insurance, ask the seller to show you proof of their insurance before you drive the car. If you don't feel comfortable about test driving the vehicle, just leave.

Let a friend or family member know beforehand where you will be, or have them come with you. You can also meet the seller in a public place, as an extra precaution.

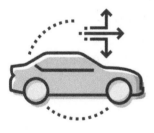

Test Drive the Car

Since you will probably have this car for a number of years, make sure that you're comfortable driving it.

Make an appointment with the dealership or seller to test drive the car. You'll need a photocopy of your driver's license and proof of insurance. To avoid a chance of

identity theft, bring your own copy of your driver's license and ask for it back when the test drive is over.

Before you get in the car:

- Check the body for any dents, cracks or rust.

- Check the windshield for any nicks or cracks.

- Check the tires for tread life and any uneven wear, which might mean that the car needs an alignment.

- Check the turn signals and brake lights.

Start the car:

- Make sure then engine runs smoothly and sounds strong. Listen for any odd noises.

- Make sure the radio works, as well as the heat and air conditioning.

- Make sure there are no warning lights on in the dashboard, and that all of the gauges work.

- Make sure that you are comfortable in the driver's seat, that there is enough leg room, enough ceiling height, and that you can see the mirrors and all of the gauges.

Take your test drive through varying conditions, like hills, stop and go traffic, and highway traffic.

- Turn off the radio, so you can listen for any odd sounds that may be warning signs.

- How is the acceleration and cornering?

- Does the car have any blind spots?

- How do the brakes work? Do they feel sticky or make a grinding noise?

- When you're on the highway, how does the car accelerate? Does it seem sluggish?

- Does the steering pull from side to side?

- When you drive up and down hills, does the car shift gears properly?

- Practice parallel parking. Does the car maneuver properly at slow speed? Is it hard to park in tight spaces?

Test Drive a Few Cars

Make sure to test drive a number of different cars, so you can best determine which one is right for you. It's a good idea to make several test drive appointments on the same day, so you can accurately compare them to one another. Also, by having another appointment to get to, you can more easily leave the dealership without feeling pressured into buying a car that day. It's smart to take some time in between the test drive and the purchase negotiations, too. You can also take the salesperson's business card and negotiate over the phone, or by email so you have a copy of your negotiations in writing.

This is a big purchase, so take your time to make sure you are making the right decision. Shopping and research will protect you from making an impulsive decision that you might regret down the road.

Check the Vehicle History Report

Once you've driven the car and you've decided that you like it, if it's a used car, get a copy of the vehicle history report. Using the vehicle identification number (VIN), you can get a copy of this report from Carfax or AutoCheck. Most dealerships will provide a copy of this report for free.

If you are considering buying a car from a personal seller, it may be worth it to purchase the vehicle history report if the owner does not supply one. This report will tell you if the car has a clean title, if the car has been in a serious accident, how many times the car has changed hands, and possibly if scheduled maintenance was performed on time.

Have Your Mechanic Inspect the Car

If you are buying a used car, especially from a private seller or an independent used car lot, you'll want to have a trusted mechanic inspect the car. It will cost around $100 to have a car inspected, but this might save you from buying a car that needs considerable amounts of repair. If

you are buying from a personal seller, you can have the seller drive the car to your mechanic for an inspection. If a dealer tries to convince you that an independent inspection is not necessary, that could be a red flag. You can insist that the car be inspected before you purchase. If you are buying from a new car dealership and the car is registered with their certified preowned (CPO) program, the car has been thoroughly inspected and might still be under warranty, so another inspection is usually not necessary.

Get Ready to Negotiate

Most experts say to negotiate on the price of the car, not the amount of the monthly payment. Just by extending the terms of the loan by another year, the monthly payment will be less but the actual cost of the financing will be higher because you'll pay more interest.

If you're already pre-approved for your loan, you're in control of the negotiations. Now that you've done your homework, you know what the ballpark pricing is for this car. You can start negotiations by making an offer that is fair, but on the low side. You can increase your offer in small increments if needed.

Make sure you ask about all taxes and fees, and get them in writing. Beware of extended warranties, extra add-ons and other potential gimmicks to increase the cost of the car.

If you're not happy with how you are being treated, leave.

 ## Buy the Car

Once you've settled on a fair price, and have all the financing worked out, you're ready to buy the car. There are a few documents that you'll need to sign or review.

Make sure to add the car to your insurance policy; you'll need proof of insurance before you drive it away.

The Sales Contract of Vehicle Purchase Agreement

Read this document carefully. Make sure that the numbers that you've discussed with the salesperson match what is on this document, since once you sign it you most likely won't be able to make any changes.

The sales contract should contain the following information:

- Vehicle sale price

- Credit for your trade-in, if you are trading in another vehicle

- Interest rate

- Length of your loan

- Add-ons, such as service contracts and extended warranties

- The amount financed

- Any rebates

- Total down payment

- Your monthly payment

- State sales tax

- Documentation fees

- Registration fees

- The Truth-in-Lending disclosure, which is federally required

The Used-Car Buyer's Guide

If you're purchasing a used car from a dealership, the car's year, make, model, vehicle identification number, and the name of the dealership is required to be displayed in the window of the vehicle. If the car is still under warranty, this buyer's guide will explain the details, including what systems are covered under the warranty, the length of the warranty, and what costs the dealer will be responsible for if repairs are needed.

Vehicle Reassignment Form/Report of Sale

This form notes the year, make and model of the vehicle, the vehicle identification number, the license plate number, if necessary, the selling price, and the mileage on the odometer. This form transfers ownership from the seller to the buyer.

Buying a Car from a Private Seller

If you are buying a car from a private seller, you need to review and sign the following:

The Car's Title. The title proves that the seller actually owns the car, and can sell it to you. If the seller does not have the title, it might mean that the seller has not paid off their loan for the car in full, and does not have the right to sell it. In this case, experts say to walk away and don't buy the car. If the seller says that they lost the title, they can apply to get a duplicate title. Don't proceed with the purchase until the seller can produce a title.

When you purchase the vehicle, sign the back of the title and have the seller sign it as well. You'll need to also record the mileage on the odometer too. If there are multiple names on the title, make sure that each seller signs the title.

Bill of Sale

The buyer or seller can also create a bill of sale. This document should include the following:

- Car year, make and model

- Vehicle identification number (VIN)

- Sale price

- Date of sale

- Names and addresses of buyer and seller

- A note that the car is "sold as is." This means that the seller makes no guarantees about the car, and that the buyer understands that no guarantees are being made.

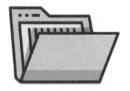

Register Your Car with the Department of Motor Vehicles

If you purchased the car from a private seller, visit the Department of Motor Vehicles to register your new car, get your license plates, and in most cases, pay taxes on your car. Bring your proof of insurance and the car's title with you. Depending on where you live, you might also need to provide a vehicle safety inspection report and an emissions test report. If you purchased your car from a dealership, these details are most likely handled by the dealership as part of the sale.

Leasing a Car

For those who want to drive a new car with a low monthly payment leasing might seem like a good option. Bear in mind, however, that when your lease is complete, you return the car to the dealer and you are left with nothing. Experts say that leasing is the most expensive way to drive in the long run, since you are driving the car at its most expensive, and you have nothing to trade in or sell at the end of your lease.

Leasing can be a good option for people who just need a car for a few years, or for those who want to drive a new car all the time, as long as they can afford the monthly payments. For those who are looking to drive inexpensively, purchasing a used car or a car without a lot of options, will be less expensive in the long run.

Leasing Terms You Should Know

Capitalized Cost (Cap-Cost): This is the price of the vehicle. This should be the Manufacturer's Suggested Retail Price (MSRP), but you can negotiate this down to a lower price with the dealer.

Capital Cost Reduction: This is your down payment. Beware of paying a large down payment. If you are not planning on purchasing the car after your lease is up, experts say to only pay a down payment if there is an incentive to do so.

Residual Value: This is the estimated price of the car once the lease is up. Cars that have a higher resale value will have lower monthly lease payments.

Factor, also called Rate or Money Factor: This is the interest rate you will pay on your loan, but unlike regular car loans it is not listed as an annual percentage rate. Multiply your

Factor by 2.4 to calculate your interest rate. Lease rates can be 2 to 3 times as high as interest rates on a car loan. You can try to negotiate your interest rate with your dealer.

Negotiate

When you're leasing a car, you can negotiate the Capitalized Cost of the car, and your interest rate factor. Remember to shop around to make sure you are getting a good deal, and don't make an impulsive decision. Read the fine print and ask questions if you don't understand any of the terms.

You Should Get Extra Insurance

In addition to regular car insurance, people who are leasing a car should consider Gap Insurance. Some lease agreements require gap insurance. This insurance covers the difference between the cash value of the car and the amount you owe on your lease. Once you drive a new car off the lot, it decreases in value considerably. If a leased car is stolen or is totaled, not having gap insurance means that your

insurance company will only pay for what the car is worth, and you will have to pay the difference.

Pay Attention to Fees

Most lease agreements are loaded with fees, some of which you can negotiate down to zero. You'll see acquisition fees, delivery charges, and disposition fees on most leases. Some also include tire fees, document fees, advertising fees and vehicle preparation fees.

Read your lease agreement carefully and try to negotiate these fees as low as possible.

Know Your Mileage

Your lease agreement will specify how many miles you can drive the car each year without incurring extra fees. If you go over this mileage, you will have to pay a fee for each extra mile you have driven. Be aware of your driving habits before you consider a lease. If you suspect that you may go over the allotment, you can negotiate the fees for extra miles, or you can pay a little extra each month so you won't be stuck with a big mileage bill at the end of your lease.

When Your Lease is Up

At the end of your lease, you can return the car to the dealership, or you might want to consider purchasing it. When your lease is up, if the vehicle is worth less than the purchase price, experts advise against purchasing it. Note that if you return the car early, before your lease is up, it is considered a default on your loan. This will negatively affect your credit, and you will still be responsible for paying the rest of your monthly payments.

Part 2: Understanding Auto Insurance

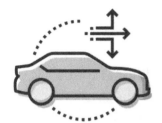

Anatomy of an Auto Insurance Policy

At its core, auto insurance is simply a contract between you and your insurance company to protect against financial loss in the unfortunate event that you have an accident. Depending on what you purchase, the insurance coverage can provide financial assistance to:

- **Repair** your vehicle or replace it in the event it is damaged or stolen

- **Reimburse** others if you cause an accident that hurts them or their vehicle

- **Pay** for any medical expenses arising from injuries you or your passengers sustain in an accident

At a minimum, most states require you to have liability insurance coverage to protect others in case you are at fault in an accident.

There are two primary kinds of liability coverage that you need:

- **Bodily Injury Liability** is coverage for injuries you might cause to someone else. Most states stipulate a minimum amount of this coverage although you can elect to purchase higher policy limits if you're willing to pay higher premiums. Table 1 on page 21 shows your state's minimum required policy limits. Note that the coverage amount for bodily injury liability is always stated using two numbers, e.g. $100,000/$300,000. The first number is the maximum amount the policy will pay for damages to one person, and the second number is the maximum amount payable for injuries for the entire accident.

- **Property Damage Liability** is coverage for damage you might cause to someone else's property. Typically this will be damage done to another person's car, but it also covers any other object you hit including buildings, fences, or street signs. Again, most states stipulate a minimum amount of this coverage per accident (see Table 1), with more coverage available at higher premiums. This number is the third one listed, immediately following the two numbers for bodily injury liability protection.

Although optional for drivers in most states, some states may require other types of coverage:

- **Medical Payments or Personal Injury Protection** (PIP) is coverage to treat injuries to you and your passengers, regardless of who is at fault in the accident. This type of coverage may also pay funeral expenses and lost wages in some circumstances. In the event that you have an accident that requires medical payments and you have this coverage, you will be required to pay a certain amount of the cost out of your own pocket, known as the deductible, and the insurance company will pay the remainder of the claim. The higher your deductible, the lower your premiums will be.

- **Under-Insured and Uninsured Motorist Coverage** is protection for you, your passengers, and your vehicle in case you have an accident with an uninsured driver, a hit-and-run driver, or a driver with insufficient insurance coverage. This type of insurance also covers you and your family members as pedestrians if you are injured by a hit-and-run driver.

Finally, there are two additional types of auto insurance to cover the cost of repairs to your car. These coverages are never required by the state, but if you have a loan or lease on your car, your lender will usually require both:

- **Collision** insurance pays to repair damage to your car from a collision, regardless of who is at fault. (In the event that you are not at fault, your insurer will generally try to get the other party's insurance company to reimburse them for the damage to your vehicle.) Collision coverage usually has a deductible between $250 and $1,000 that you must pay toward the repairs before your insurer will pay its portion. As with PIP, the higher your deductible, the lower your premiums will be.

- **Comprehensive insurance** covers your car for everything that is not covered by collision insurance. This includes the cost to replace or repair your vehicle due to theft or damage from things like hail, water, flood, fire, wind, explosion, earthquake, animals, or vandalism. This coverage also has a deductible, which is usually equal to or lower than the deductible on your collision insurance.

Additional Types of Coverage Available to You

In addition to the basic components listed above, insurance companies also offer other add-on coverage to enhance their customers' policies. These often include:

- **Roadside Assistance** pays for towing charges up to a certain limit. It also includes labor costs for breakdowns that can be repaired on site. If you own an older car that is more prone to breakdown, this type of insurance may be attractive. However, this coverage is not necessary if you already have an auto club membership.

- **Rental Car Reimbursement** pays for the cost of a rental car while your car is being repaired after an accident. The coverage is usually limited to $30 per day, but can vary by insurer. Keep in mind that this type of insurance will not pay for a

rental car when yours is in for regular maintenance or repairs unrelated to an accident. It is strictly an add-on to your collision or comprehensive coverage to help you get your car back in working order.

Depending upon your family's vehicle situation, this may or may not be necessary.

- **Gap Insurance for Leased or Financed Vehicles** covers the difference between what the insurance company will pay and the amount you owe on a leased or financed vehicle in the event it is damaged beyond repair. Not all companies offer this coverage. However, some auto leases actually include it as a part of your lease agreement, so be sure to check your lease documents before purchasing this add-on coverage.

Coverage Required in Your State

Every state has a financial responsibility law requiring its residents to show proof of their ability to pay for any claims arising from an accident, up to a certain amount.

As you might expect, most people purchase auto insurance simply to comply with these laws, sticking with the bare minimum coverage limits mandated by their state. Table 1 on the following page provides a list of the current liability policy limits required by each state.

Note that the liability limits are shown in a series of three numbers.

- The first number refers to the maximum amount the insurer will pay for one individual's bodily injury.

- The second number refers to the maximum amount the insurer will pay for all people injured in an accident.

- And the third number refers to the maximum amount of property damage the insurer will pay for. For example, Alabama's limits of 25/50/25 mean that Alabama requires its residents to purchase at least

$25,000 of bodily injury coverage for one person, at least $50,000 of bodily injury coverage for all parties injured in a single accident, and at least $25,000 of property damage coverage.

These figures represent the minimum amount of coverage you must purchase, but they are also the maximum amount your insurer will have to pay in the event of an accident.

So, what happens if you purchase the bare minimum required but cause an accident where the costs exceed these limits?

In that case, the other party may sue you to collect what your insurance company did not pay. If you don't have many assets, this may not be a concern for you. Otherwise, you may find it worthwhile to purchase higher policy limits than the minimums required by your state. In fact, most insurers and consumer groups recommend drivers hold minimum liability coverage of $100,000 per person and $300,000 per accident for bodily injury. This is usually combined with a $100,000 limit for property damage given the high cost of many cars these days, plus the potential for damaging other types of property at the accident scene.

Table 1. Automobile Financial Responsibility Limits and Enforcement By State

State	Insurance Required (1)	Liability Limits (2)	State	Insurance Required (1)	Liability Limits (2)
Alabama	BI & PD Liab	25/50/25	Nebraska	BI & PD Liab, UM, UIM	25/50/25
Alaska	BI & PD Liab	50/100/25	Nevada	BI & PD Liab	25/50/20
Arizona	BI & PD Liab	15/30/10	New Hampshire	FR only	25/50/25
Arkansas	BI & PD Liab, PIP	25/50/25	New Jersey	BI & PD Liab, PIP, UM, UIM	15/30/5 (6)
California	BI & PD Liab	15/30/5 (3)	New Mexico	BI & PD Liab	25/50/10
Colorado	BI & PD Liab	25/50/15	New York	BI & PD Liab, PIP, UM	25/50/10 (7)
Connecticut	BI & PD Liab, UM, UIM	25/50/20	North Carolina	BI & PD Liab, UM, UIM	30/60/25
Delaware	BI & PD Liab, PIP	25/50/10	North Dakota	BI & PD Liab, PIP, UM, UIM	25/50/25
Florida	PD Liab, PIP	10/20/10 (4)	Ohio	BI & PD Liab	25/50/25
Georgia	BI & PD Liab	25/50/25	Oklahoma	BI & PD Liab	25/50/25
Hawaii	BI & PD Liab, PIP	20/40/10	Oregon	BI & PD Liab, PIP, UM, UIM	25/50/20
Idaho	BI & PD Liab	25/50/15	Pennsylvania	BI & PD Liab, PIP	15/30/5
Illinois	BI & PD Liab, UM, UIM	25/50/20	Rhode Island	BI & PD Liab	25/50/25
Indiana	BI & PD Liab	25/50/25*	South Carolina	BI & PD Liab, UM	25/50/25
Iowa	BI & PD Liab	20/40/15	South Dakota	BI & PD Liab, UM, UIM	25/50/25
Kansas	BI & PD Liab, PIP	25/50/25	Tennessee	BI & PD Liab	25/50/15 (4)
Kentucky	BI & PD Liab, PIP, UM, UIM	25/50/25 (4)	Texas	BI & PD Liab	30/60/25
Louisiana	BI & PD Liab	15/30/25	Utah	BI & PD Liab, PIP	25/65/15 (4)
Maine	BI & PD Liab, UM, UIM, Medpay	50/100/25 (5)	Vermont	BI & PD Liab, PIP	25/50/10
Maryland	BI & PD Liab, PIP, UM, UIM	30/60/15	Virginia	BI & PD Liab (9), UM, UIM	25/50/20
Massachusetts	BI & PD Liab, PIP, UM	20/40/5	Washington	BI & PD Liab	25/50/10
Michigan	BI & PD Liab, PIP	20/40/10	Wash. D.C.	BI & PD Liab, PIP, UM	25/50/10
Minnesota	BI & PD Liab, PIP, UM, UIM	30/60/10	West Virginia	BI & PD Liab, UM, UIM	20/50/25
Mississippi	BI & PD Liab	25/50/25	Wisconsin	BI & PD Liab, UM, Medpay	25/50/10
Missouri	BI & PD Liab, UM	25/50/10	Wyoming	BI & PD Liab	25/50/20
Montana	BI & PD Liab	25/50/20			

1. Compulsory Coverage:
   BI Liab = Bodily injury liability   **Med** = First party (policyholder) medical expenses
   PD Liab = Property damage liability   **UIM** = Underinsured Motorist
   UM = Uninsured motorist   **PD** = Physical damage
   PIP = Personal Injury Protection. Mandatory in no-fault states. Includes medical, rehabilitation, loss of earnings and funeral expenses. In some states PIP includes essential services such as child care
   FR = Financial responsibility only. Insurance not compulsory

(continued on next page)

2. The first two numbers refer to bodily injury liability limits and the third number to property damage liability. For example, 20/40/10 means coverage up to $40,000 for all persons injured in an accident, subject to a limit of $20,000 for one individual, and $10,000 coverage for property damage

3. a. Insurer must notify Department of Motor Vehicles or other state agency of cancellation or nonrenewal.
    b. Insurer must verify financial responsibility or insurance after an accident or arrest.
    c. Insurer must verify randomly selected insurance policies upon request.
    d. Includes states where law allows an online web-based verification system where administrators can verify insurance compliance in real time.

4. Low-cost policy limits for low-income drivers in the California Automobile Assigned Risk Plan are 10/20/3

5. Instead of policy limits, policyholders can satisfy the requirement with a combined single limit policy. Amounts vary by state

6. In addition, policyholders must also have coverage for medical payments. Amounts vary by state

7. Basic policy (optional) limits are 10/10/5. Uninsured and underinsured motorist coverage not available under the basic policy but uninsured motorist coverage is required under the standard policy. Special Automobile Insurance Policy available for certain drives which only covers emergency treatment and a $10,000 death benefit

8. In addition, policyholders must have 50/100 for wrongful death coverage.

9. UIM Mandatory in policies with UM limits exceeding certain limits. Amount vary by state.

10. Compulsory to buy insurance or pay an Uninsured Motorists Vehicle (UMV) fee to the state Department of Motor Vehicles.

Data in this table effective January 2019

Source: Property Casualty Insurers Association of America; state departments of insurance and motor vehicles. (www.iii.org).

 ## "No-Fault" Insurance

Aside from specifying required liability limits, some states also have what is known as a "no-fault" liability law.

In such states, each person in an accident is covered by their own insurance company, regardless of who caused the accident. Although you may feel such a system is unfair if you are not the one who caused the accident, you will undoubtedly appreciate the ease with which you can file a claim since you're only dealing with your own insurance company. Plus, this system helps to lower insurance costs and keep policy costs down by eliminating most small court claims and limiting lawsuits to only those involving serious injuries.

Twelve states currently require all auto policies to be no-fault policies:

- Florida
- Hawaii
- Kansas
- Kentucky
- Massachusetts
- Michigan
- Minnesota
- New Jersey
- New York
- North Dakota
- Pennsylvania
- Utah

In these states, if you have no-fault insurance, you are immune from being sued and from suing other drivers for non-economic damages like pain and suffering. However, if you have traditional liability coverage, you can sue and be sued if the other driver also has traditional coverage.

Because "no-fault" insurance provides immunity from being sued, it tends to be the choice of bad drivers. Even so, these same limits on lawsuits also tend to make no-fault coverage the cheaper option. Consequently, this system is often charged with unfairly punishing good drivers.

Eleven states allow you to add a no-fault provision to your auto insurance policy in order to facilitate claims, but do not restrict your ability to sue the other party in an accident.

These states, known as "Add-On" states, are:

- Arkansas
- Delaware
- D.C.
- Maryland
- New Hampshire
- Oregon
- South Dakota
- Texas
- Virginia
- Washington
- Wisconsin

In addition, drivers in the District of Columbia can choose no-fault or a traditional liability policy, but if they choose no-fault, they have 60 days after an accident to decide if they want the no-fault benefits or wish to pursue a claim against the other person in the accident.

The remaining 27 states have regular liability policies with no specific limitations on your ability to sue for damages.

Things Your Policy Won't Cover

In addition to stating the types of injury or damage that are covered, your auto insurance policy will also have a list of things that are not covered, called "exclusions." The most common exclusions are:

- **Intentional Injury**

  Your policy will not pay for damages if you intentionally hit another vehicle or piece of property.

- **Property Owned or Transported**

  This refers to personal items carried in your vehicle. For example, if you are carrying golf clubs in your car and they are damaged during an accident, your auto policy will not pay to repair or replace them. However, your homeowners policy may provide such coverage.

- **Public or Livery Conveyance**

  If you use your car to transport people or property for a fee (e.g. as a taxi), your car will not be covered under your personal auto policy. Instead, you would need to purchase a separate commercial auto policy. This exclusion doesn't apply to car pools.

- **Other Business Uses**

  Even if you run a business that doesn't involve transporting people or property, your car will not be covered under your personal auto policy when it is being used for business purposes. You would instead need to purchase a separate commercial auto policy.

- **Motorized Vehicles with Fewer than Four Wheels**

  Motorcycles, mopeds, scooters, all-terrain vehicles, snowmobiles, and other similar-type vehicles are not automatically covered under your auto policy. However, coverage for these vehicles may generally be added onto your policy for an additional fee.

Insuring Your Other Vehicles

Auto insurance policies are designed to only cover your personal car or truck. Nevertheless, you can usually add other coverage's to an auto policy for other forms of transportation such as a motorcycle, all-terrain vehicle, recreational vehicle (RV), snowmobile, jet ski, or boat. Adding coverage for any of these vehicles is known as attaching a "rider" onto your auto policy.

Collector and antique cars also require special coverage, but this is usually a bit harder to get. Many companies won't insure vehicles more than 20 years old, except possibly on a rider with restricted usage. That's not to say that you won't be able to find coverage. In fact, some insurers specialize in high value collector and antique vehicles that are used infrequently. You just won't be able to add such coverage onto the policy covering your everyday vehicle. If you own a collector or antique automobile, contact your local car club and they should be able to recommend an agent to assist you with this coverage.

Exotic, high-performance, and high-value vehicle owners may also have trouble finding coverage. For example, there are not a lot of insurance companies that want to take on the risk of a Ferrari, Rolls Royce, or Bentley since the cost to repair or replace them is so high. If you own a car of this type, contact an insurance agent (or possibly your auto dealer) for assistance in finding insurance coverage.

How Premiums are Determined

Insurance companies take a wide range of factors into consideration when determining how much you will have to pay in premiums. These include:

- **Amount of Coverage Purchased**

  The higher the policy's maximum coverage limits, the higher your premium will be. You may be able to get away with the minimums required by your state, but ask for pricing on higher limits before making that decision. Depending on the other factors listed below, you may be able to substantially increase your

protection for a very modest increase in your premiums.

- **Amount of Deductible**

  The deductible is the portion of the claim you must pay before the insurance company will pay the remainder. Deductibles typically range from $250 to $1,000. As you might expect, the higher the deductible, the lower your premium will be. (This applies to collision, comprehensive, and personal injury protection.)

- **Type of Car**

  After the amount of coverage you purchase, the type of car you drive is the second most important factor in determining your premium. Due to the nature of their drivers, owning a sports car will usually drive up your insurance premium. Likewise, sport utility vehicles (SUVs) are usually more expensive to insure while family sedans are usually less expensive to insure. This varies somewhat by insurer based on each insurer's own assessment of the cost to repair the vehicle, its safety features, and its propensity for being stolen.

- **Driving History**

  The insurance company uses your driving record as an indication of the type of driver you are for determining how much risk they are accepting. Therefore, if you have a history of auto insurance claims or traffic violations, your insurer will consider you a higher risk driver and will raise your premium rate accordingly.

  Drivers with very poor records or a DUI conviction can even have difficulty finding an insurer who will cover them at all. If you fall into this category, you may have to turn to your state's Assigned Risk Plan - there's one in every state - which assigns you to an insurer. The state will require that insurer to provide you with coverage but will also allow them to charge you significantly higher rates.

- **Gender**

  Statistically speaking, men have more accidents than women. As such, men tend to be charged higher premiums.

- **Age**

  Statistics again indicate that younger and older drivers tend to be the riskiest. In 2017 drivers age 16 to 20 years old accounted for 5.3 percent of all the drivers involved in fatal crashes and 35.6 percent of all the drivers involved in all police-reported crashes.[1] If you are a young driver, expect to pay higher premiums. This becomes less of a factor at age 21 and is removed as a factor at age 25, after which you'll enjoy many years before you grow old enough for your insurer to consider you high risk once again. Premiums begin to creep up again for older drivers, as statistics support their riskier status. According to the National Highway Traffic Safety Administration, 12.1% of all people killed on the road in 2017 were 65 or older.

- **Marital Status**

  Married people tend to have fewer accidents than single people, so you will likely see a discount in your premium if you are married.

---

[1] Insurance Information Institute (www.iii.org)

- **Other Drivers in your Household**

   When determining your premium, your insurer will not only look at all of the above factors for you, it will also take these factors into consideration for everyone in your household (any other licensed drivers in your house must be disclosed on your application). That means a teenage son would bring your premium way up, but a spouse with a clean driving record would help bring the premium down.

- **Location**

   Insurers must get their premium rates approved in each state where they are licensed, leading to a variation in rates between states based on the insurer's claims history in the state. For example, drivers in Florida have more accidents than drivers in Wyoming, so Florida drivers pay higher premium rates - even for the same insurer insuring the same driver and vehicle. And within Florida, there are some areas that have more accidents than others (e.g., highly urban areas like Miami) which lead to even higher rates for drivers located within those areas.

- **Vehicle Usage**

   The more you drive, the more opportunity there is for you to be in an accident. Therefore, you'll find the premiums lower for your "weekend car" than for a car you use to drive 30 miles each way to work. The more you drive the vehicle, the higher the premiums will be.

- **Credit Scores**

   Insurance companies have recently started using credit scores as a predictor of future claims activity. There has been much debate about the validity of this factor, but research, including a 2003 study by EPIC Actuaries, that show a correlation between credit scores and claims activity. The law does not allow an insurer to use your credit history as the sole factor in determining your premiums. Your credit score can, however, be used against you to decline coverage or as one of several factors used to set your premium. Not all companies use credit scores, so if your credit history is particularly bad, it is all the more important that you shop around for an auto policy from an insurer that does not use credit scores as a factor in setting its premiums. This could easily save you hundreds of dollars per year.

Although these are the basic factors that every insurance company uses in setting its premiums, the amount you pay will still vary from company to company based upon each insurer's underwriting model (the process of assessing your risk and pricing your policy accordingly). Some insurance companies weight some factors more heavily than others.

In addition, one company may have had a high level of claims in a particular state, forcing it to raise premiums in that state, whereas another company in the same state may have had a low level of claims there, allowing them to lower premiums in that state.

Also, some insurers charge a flat fee for your liability coverage, regardless of the vehicle you drive, while others base your premium for liability coverage on the type of vehicle.

Ways to Save Money on Your Premium

The most effective way to save money on your auto insurance premium is to be a safe driver. The fewer accidents and traffic violations you have, the more insurers

you'll have bidding for your business and the lower their rate quotes will be. Other ways to lower your premium are to:

- **Take a Driver Safety Course**

  If you've been ticketed for an accident or some other violation, the state will remove it from your driving record when you take a driver safety course. The required courses vary from state to state and can help to keep your driving record as clean as possible. In addition, almost all insurance companies will lower your premium just for taking it. So, even if you haven't been ticketed, you can still take a driver safety course to save money.

- **Increase your Deductible**

  Ask your insurer for premium quotes using different deductible levels to see how much you could save by covering a greater portion of an accident cost out of your own pocket. It may be worth it to go with a higher deductible, particularly if you're a safe driver who is less likely to be in an accident or if you've got the financial capacity to pay a higher deductible in the event of an accident.

- **Forego Comprehensive and/or Collision Coverage**

  If the value of your vehicle is not that high, you might want to consider going without comprehensive and/or collision coverage. For instance, if your car is more than ten years old or if it already has significant body damage, the cost of these coverages over a year or two could exceed the value of the vehicle entirely.

- **Compare Prices Regularly**

  Shop your policy around by getting premium quotes from other insurers every year or two. You don't necessarily have to change companies, but this is generally a worthwhile exercise. It's relatively easy to do and you could find another insurer that will save you a significant amount of money on your auto insurance.

- **Use the Same Company for Homeowners and Auto Insurance**

  Almost all insurers will give you a discount on your premium if you purchase insurance for both your home and your car from them. But, even with this discount, you could end up paying more than you would by shopping for the least

expensive coverage from two separate, unrelated insurers.

- **Take Advantage of Group Discounts**

  If you are a member of a national group like AAA, AARP, AMA, ABA, etc. ask your agent if there are any special discounts for your group. And if you or your parents were in the military, be sure to get a rate quote from USAA, a company that specifically caters to military personnel. As with other discounts, you'll want to make sure that the discounted policy is indeed less expensive than your other alternatives. In other words, don't buy it just because the insurer is giving a discount to your group.

- **Choose a Vehicle that is Less Expensive to Insure**

  When you're in the process of buying a new car, that is the perfect time to factor insurance costs into your selection decision. Ask your insurer (as well as other insurers) for premium quotes on a couple of different vehicles that you are considering so you can see if one would cost you more from an insurance standpoint. Premiums are generally lower for small sedans, minivans, and mid-sized family sedans than they are for sports cars and large SUVs. Also, make sure your prospective purchase isn't high on the stolen vehicle list since insurers use this list heavily in setting their premium rates. See Table 2 for the most and least expensive vehicles to insure.

- **Choose a Hybrid Vehicle**

  Some insurers offer discounted insurance rates to hybrid drivers in some states. Research shows that hybrid drivers pose a lower insurance risk because they drive fewer miles and have better driving pattern and record. Make sure to inquire about how choosing a hybrid might save you money.

- **Explore Usage Based Insurance (UBI) Options**

  Insurers are increasingly using new technology to determine how safely the car is being driven and to gather data on driving habits. Insurance companies offer programs that focus solely on miles driven or tracks driving behavior as well as miles driven. Your miles driven, time of day and hard braking data is tracked by installing an electronic device in your car and may result in lower insurance rates for safe driving. Ask about these voluntary programs when you shop for auto insurance.

Table 2. 10 Most and Least Expensive 2020 Vehicles to Insure[2]

Most Expensive	Least Expensive
1. Mercedes AMG GT-R	1. Mazda CX-3 Sport
2. Audi R8 5.2L V10 Quattro	2. Honda CR-V LX
3. Nissan GT-R	3. Wrangler Sport X
4. BMW M8	4. Subaru Outback 2.51
5. Mercedes S65 AMG	5. Fiat 500X Pop
6. BMW M760i XDrive	6. Honda Odyssey LX
7. Porsche Panamera GTS Turbo	7. Subaru Forester 2.5l
8. Tesla Model X Performance	8. Mazda CX=5
9. Dodge Challenger SRT Hellcat	9. Jeep Renegade Sport
10. Mercedes S560 Convertible	10. Honda HR-V LX

[2] Source: Insure.com.

- **Use your Clean Credit Report to your Advantage**

  Depending upon the laws in your state, insurance companies can use your credit history to grant or deny coverage or as a factor in setting your premium rate. So be sure to get a copy of your credit report and make sure any erroneous information is removed (this is a good idea even when you're not shopping for auto insurance). You'll usually be given the option of whether or not to grant the insurance company access to your credit report. So, if you have decent credit, let them see it and it could save you some money.

- **Ask About Discounts Specifically for Young Drivers**

  If you have a young driver in your house, be sure to ask if your insurer gives any discounts for taking a drivers' education course or getting good grades. Such discounts are becoming more popular these days and companies attempt to better assess their risk of an accident.

- **Pay your Premium in Advance**

  If you can afford it, pay your full annual or semiannual policy premium up front. Some

companies actually give you a discount for doing so, while others will charge an extra fee ($3 to $5 each month) if you elect to pay your premiums monthly.

With the growth of the Internet, there is a wealth of additional free information available to help you save money or get better coverage on your auto insurance. See the Appendix for a listing of useful websites.

How to Shop for an Auto Policy

Now that you realize the value of shopping around to get the best rate on your auto insurance policy, the next step is to take action. There are three possible routes to go - agents, direct writers, and the Internet - and you should feel free to pursue any or all of them depending on the amount of time and effort you're willing to devote.

Agents

Most people prefer face-to-face interaction and therefore opt to work with an insurance agent. There are pros and cons to this approach, however. On the positive side, a knowledgeable agent can walk you through the entire purchasing process, answering any questions you may have and helping you to select the policy components that are right for you. An agent can also be particularly helpful when you have a claim by assisting you in your dealings with the claims adjuster and the insurance company.

On the downside, not all insurance agents are created equal. Some have lousy customer service, essentially negating the benefits listed above. And others are so focused on increasing their commissions that they try to push you into coverage that you really don't need. Plus, policies available through an agent are generally more expensive than those available through direct writers or the Internet due to the cost of paying the agent's commission.

Finding a good agent is pretty much a hit and miss proposition. Your best bet is to rely on referrals from friends, neighbors, and family members who are happy with their insurance agent.

You can also consult your local phone book or do an Internet search to identify more names even though you won't have any information on their quality.

Keep in mind that there are actually two types of insurance agents: exclusive agents that represent only one company and independent agents that represent many companies. If you find an agent who

works with only one company, you'll definitely want to check premium prices elsewhere before selecting an insurer to go with. And even if you're working with an independent agent who represents multiple companies, it still doesn't hurt to comparison shop with other agents or on the Internet to make sure you're getting the best deal possible.

Bottom line: If your preference is to have someone else do most of the legwork, an agent is your best bet, particularly if he has more than one company to choose from.

Direct Writers

Some insurance companies cut out the middle man (i.e., the agent) and instead employ their own salespeople who perform the agent's functions via phone. These companies are called direct writers. Shopping for a policy from a direct writer can be time consuming since you essentially have to call each company one by one to get a premium quote. At the same time though, some of the best deals can be found through direct writers due to their lower cost structure. You won't get quite the same personalized service as dealing with an agent, but the saving could make the impersonalization worth it to you.

Most direct writers advertise heavily in the mail, on the radio, and on television, so you've probably seen something from at least one of them without realizing you were being solicited by a direct writer. Also, some have started selling their policies through agents and then adding the agent's commission directly onto the premium you pay. Consult the Appendix for a list of websites operated by insurance companies some of which are direct writers.

The Internet

The Internet is a great place to do your comparison shopping. There are a large number of websites that can search through hundreds of insurers to find which ones offer the lowest premiums based on your specific situation. What's more, you can usually get a premium quote immediately after entering some information about yourself. Some insurance websites require you to give them a great deal of information up front such as your driver's license number, your social security number, the vehicle identification number (VIN#) of your vehicle, and information about any past accidents or traffic violations. This can be a lot of work, particularly if you do it for multiple policy searches. Other websites request only basic information in order to give you a ballpark quote. From there, you can decide if it's worth your time to enter all of the details required to get an actual quote.

 If you want to get the rock bottom, lowest price possible on your auto insurance and you have the time to devote to it, the Internet is probably your best option. You won't have the comfort of consulting with an agent or even dealing with a salesperson. On the other hand, you'll be able to proceed at your own pace, from the comfort of your own home, without anyone pushing you to buy more.

Finding a website that sells auto insurance is extremely easy. All you have to do is put "auto insurance quotes" into a search engine and you'll get more than you can possibly use. For your convenience, we've also included the web address for some of the major online vendors of auto insurance in the Appendix of this publication.

In order to cut down on the time involved with shopping for insurance on the Internet, be sure to supply the most accurate information possible. Your driving record and the history of your vehicle will be scrutinized before a policy is issued, so it won't do you any good to try and skirt any blemishes. It will only make the process longer.

When shopping for an auto insurance policy, we recommend you follow these steps:

Step 1

Gather all of the personal information that will be needed in order to receive a premium quote. This includes your:

- Driver's license number
- Social security number
- Vehicle make and model
- Vehicle Identification number (VIN#) located on your registration or inside door panel
- Driving history for the last five years, including any accidents or traffic citations
- Policy limits and deductibles on your current auto policy

Step 2

Consult with your friends, neighbors, and family members to see who they use for their auto insurance and what their level of satisfaction has been.

Step 3

Decide which avenue(s) you'd like to use to shop for your new policy: an agent, a direct writer, or the Internet.

Step 4

Give some consideration to the types of coverage you are interested in purchasing as well as the policy limits for your liability coverage and the deductibles for your collision and comprehensive coverage. You can always request quotes for multiple options, but it's good to have an idea of what you want going in.

Step 5

Set aside some dedicated, uninterrupted time and contact the agents, companies, or websites you've decided to pursue. A good plan of action will help cut down on the amount of time involved.

Step 6

Take good notes so you can make sure you are getting "apples-to-apples" comparisons and so you will know who to contact if you should select a particular policy. There is a Premium Quote Comparison Worksheet in the Appendix to help you with this process.

Step 7

Narrow your list down to the least expensive two or three quotes and then take a look at those specific companies in more detail.

Specifically, check:

- Each company's Weiss Safety Rating at https://greyhouse.weissratings.com to make sure the company is financially sound and will be around to pay your claim if you have one. See the Weiss Recommended Auto Insurers.

- Contact your state department of insurance to see if they can provide you with any information on the companies' history of consumer complaints or anything else that may aid you in your decision-making process.

- Conduct a search on the Internet using the company name. This may turn up postings from others that could be helpful to you.

Step 8

Select a company and submit an application to purchase your policy. If the paperwork comes back with a premium quote that differs from what you were originally quoted, don't hesitate about moving on to your second choice of companies.

Weiss Ratings' Recommended Auto Insurers by State

The following pages list Weiss Ratings' Recommended Auto Insurers (based strictly on financial safety) licensed to do business in each state. These insurers currently receive a Weiss Safety Rating of A+, A, A-, or B+, indicating their strong financial position. Companies are listed by their Safety Rating and then alphabetically within each Safety Rating grouping.

If an insurer is not on this list, it should not be automatically assumed that the firm is weak. Indeed, there are many firms that have not achieved a B+ or better rating but are in relatively good condition with adequate resources to cover their risk. Not being included in this list should not be construed as a recommendation to cancel a policy.

To get Weiss Safety Rating for a company not included here, or to check the latest rating for these companies, go to https://greyhouse.weissratings.com.

Weiss Safety Rating	Our rating is measured on a scale from A to F and considers a wide range of factors. Highly rated companies are, in our opinion, less likely to experience financial difficulties than lower-rated firms. See "What Our Ratings Mean" in the Appendix for a definition of each rating category.
Name	The insurance company's legally registered name, which can sometimes differ from the name that the company uses for advertising. An insurer's name can be very similar to the name of other companies which may not be on this list, so make sure you note the exact name before contacting your agent.
City, Address, State	The address of the main office where you can contact the firm for additional information or for the location of local branches and/or registered agents.
Telephone	The telephone number to call for information on purchasing an insurance policy from the company.

The following list of recommended Auto Insurers by State is based on ratings as of the date of publication. Visit https://greyhouse.weissratings.com to check the latest rating of these companies.

Alabama

B+

Name	City	Address	State	Zip	Telephone
Geico General Ins Co	Chevy Chase	5260 Western Avenue	MD	20815	800-841-3000
USAA General Indemnity Co	San Antonio	9800 Fredericksburg Road	TX	78288	210-498-1411

Arizona

B+

Name	City	Address	State	Zip	Telephone
American Family Mutl Ins Co SI	Madison	6000 American Parkway	WI	53783	608-249-2111
American Standard Ins Co of WI	Madison	6000 American Parkway	WI	53783	608-249-2111
Geico General Ins Co	Chevy Chase	5260 Western Avenue	MD	20815	800-841-3000
USAA General Indemnity Co	San Antonio	9800 Fredericksburg Road	TX	78288	210-498-1411

Arkansas

B+

Name	City	Address	State	Zip	Telephone
Geico General Ins Co	Chevy Chase	5260 Western Avenue	MD	20815	800-841-3000
USAA General Indemnity Co	San Antonio	9800 Fredericksburg Road	TX	78288	210-498-1411

California

B+

Name	City	Address	State	Zip	Telephone
Geico General Ins Co	Chevy Chase	5260 Western Avenue	MD	20815	800-841-3000
Interins Exchange	Costa Mesa	3333 Fairview Road	CA	92626	714-850-5111
USAA General Indemnity Co	San Antonio	9800 Fredericksburg Road	TX	78288	210-498-1411

Colorado

B+

Name	City	Address	State	Zip	Telephone
American Family Mutl Ins Co SI	Madison	6000 American Parkway	WI	53783	608-249-2111
American Standard Ins Co of WI	Madison	6000 American Parkway	WI	53783	608-249-2111
Geico General Ins Co	Chevy Chase	5260 Western Avenue	MD	20815	800-841-3000
USAA General Indemnity Co	San Antonio	9800 Fredericksburg Road	TX	78288	210-498-1411

Connecticut

B+

Name	City	Address	State	Zip	Telephone
Geico General Ins Co	Chevy Chase	5260 Western Avenue	MD	20815	800-841-3000
USAA General Indemnity Co	San Antonio	9800 Fredericksburg Road	TX	78288	210-498-1411

Delaware

B+

Name	City	Address	State	Zip	Telephone
Geico General Ins Co	Chevy Chase	5260 Western Avenue	MD	20815	800-841-3000
USAA General Indemnity Co	San Antonio	9800 Fredericksburg Road	TX	78288	210-498-1411

District of Columbia

B+

Name	City	Address	State	Zip	Telephone
Geico General Ins Co	Chevy Chase	5260 Western Avenue	MD	20815	800-841-3000
USAA General Indemnity Co	San Antonio	9800 Fredericksburg Road	TX	78288	210-498-1411

Florida

B+

Name	City	Address	State	Zip	Telephone
Geico General Ins Co	Chevy Chase	5260 Western Avenue	MD	20815	800-841-3000
USAA General Indemnity Co	San Antonio	9800 Fredericksburg Road	TX	78288	210-498-1411

Georgia

B+

Name	City	Address	State	Zip	Telephone
Geico General Ins Co	Chevy Chase	5260 Western Avenue	MD	20815	800-841-3000
USAA General Indemnity Co	San Antonio	9800 Fredericksburg Road	TX	78288	210-498-1411

Hawaii

B+

Name	City	Address	State	Zip	Telephone
Interins Exchange	Costa Mesa	3333 Fairview Road	CA	92626	714-850-5111
National Casualty Co	Columbus	1 W Nationwide Blvd 1-04-701	OH	43215	480-365-4000
USAA General Indemnity Co	San Antonio	9800 Fredericksburg Road	TX	78288	210-498-1411

Idaho

B+

Name	City	Address	State	Zip	Telephone
American Family Mutl Ins Co SI	Madison	6000 American Parkway	WI	53783	608-249-2111
American Standard Ins Co of WI	Madison	6000 American Parkway	WI	53783	608-249-2111
Geico General Ins Co	Chevy Chase	5260 Western Avenue	MD	20815	800-841-3000
USAA General Indemnity Co	San Antonio	9800 Fredericksburg Road	TX	78288	210-498-1411

Illinois

B+

Name	City	Address	State	Zip	Telephone
American Family Mutl Ins Co SI	Madison	6000 American Parkway	WI	53783	608-249-2111
American Standard Ins Co of WI	Madison	6000 American Parkway	WI	53783	608-249-2111
Geico General Ins Co	Chevy Chase	5260 Western Avenue	MD	20815	800-841-3000
USAA General Indemnity Co	San Antonio	9800 Fredericksburg Road	TX	78288	210-498-1411

Indiana

B+

Name	City	Address	State	Zip	Telephone
American Family Mutl Ins Co SI	Madison	6000 American Parkway	WI	53783	608-249-2111
American Standard Ins Co of WI	Madison	6000 American Parkway	WI	53783	608-249-2111
Geico General Ins Co	Chevy Chase	5260 Western Avenue	MD	20815	800-841-3000
USAA General Indemnity Co	San Antonio	9800 Fredericksburg Road	TX	78288	210-498-1411

Iowa

B+

Name	City	Address	State	Zip	Telephone
American Family Mutl Ins Co SI	Madison	6000 American Parkway	WI	53783	608-249-2111
American Standard Ins Co of WI	Madison	6000 American Parkway	WI	53783	608-249-2111
Geico General Ins Co	Chevy Chase	5260 Western Avenue	MD	20815	800-841-3000
USAA General Indemnity Co	San Antonio	9800 Fredericksburg Road	TX	78288	210-498-1411

Kansas

B+

Name	City	Address	State	Zip	Telephone
American Family Mutl Ins Co SI	Madison	6000 American Parkway	WI	53783	608-249-2111
American Standard Ins Co of WI	Madison	6000 American Parkway	WI	53783	608-249-2111
Geico General Ins Co	Chevy Chase	5260 Western Avenue	MD	20815	800-841-3000
USAA General Indemnity Co	San Antonio	9800 Fredericksburg Road	TX	78288	210-498-1411

Kentucky

B+

Name	City	Address	State	Zip	Telephone
Geico General Ins Co	Chevy Chase	5260 Western Avenue	MD	20815	800-841-3000
USAA General Indemnity Co	San Antonio	9800 Fredericksburg Road	TX	78288	210-498-1411

Louisiana

B+

Name	City	Address	State	Zip	Telephone
Geico General Ins Co	Chevy Chase	5260 Western Avenue	MD	20815	800-841-3000
USAA General Indemnity Co	San Antonio	9800 Fredericksburg Road	TX	78288	210-498-1411

Maine

B+

Name	City	Address	State	Zip	Telephone
Geico General Ins Co	Chevy Chase	5260 Western Avenue	MD	20815	800-841-3000
Interins Exchange	Costa Mesa	3333 Fairview Road	CA	92626	714-850-5111
USAA General Indemnity Co	San Antonio	9800 Fredericksburg Road	TX	78288	210-498-1411

Maryland

B+

Name	City	Address	State	Zip	Telephone
Geico General Ins Co	Chevy Chase	5260 Western Avenue	MD	20815	800-841-3000
USAA General Indemnity Co	San Antonio	9800 Fredericksburg Road	TX	78288	210-498-1411

Massachusetts

B+

Name	City	Address	State	Zip	Telephone
Geico General Ins Co	Chevy Chase	5260 Western Avenue	MD	20815	800-841-3000
USAA General Indemnity Co	San Antonio	9800 Fredericksburg Road	TX	78288	210-498-1411

Minnesota

B+

Name	City	Address	State	Zip	Telephone
American Family Mutl Ins Co SI	Madison	6000 American Parkway	WI	53783	608-249-2111
American Standard Ins Co of WI	Madison	6000 American Parkway	WI	53783	608-249-2111
Geico General Ins Co	Chevy Chase	5260 Western Avenue	MD	20815	800-841-3000
USAA General Indemnity Co	San Antonio	9800 Fredericksburg Road	TX	78288	210-498-1411

Mississippi

B+

Name	City	Address	State	Zip	Telephone
Geico General Ins Co	Chevy Chase	5260 Western Avenue	MD	20815	800-841-3000
USAA General Indemnity Co	San Antonio	9800 Fredericksburg Road	TX	78288	210-498-1411

Missouri

B+

Name	City	Address	State	Zip	Telephone
American Family Mutl Ins Co SI	Madison	6000 American Parkway	WI	53783	608-249-2111
American Standard Ins Co of WI	Madison	6000 American Parkway	WI	53783	608-249-2111
Geico General Ins Co	Chevy Chase	5260 Western Avenue	MD	20815	800-841-3000
USAA General Indemnity Co	San Antonio	9800 Fredericksburg Road	TX	78288	210-498-1411

Montana

B+

Name	City	Address	State	Zip	Telephone
Geico General Ins Co	Chevy Chase	5260 Western Avenue	MD	20815	800-841-3000
USAA General Indemnity Co	San Antonio	9800 Fredericksburg Road	TX	78288	210-498-1411

Nebraska

B+

Name	City	Address	State	Zip	Telephone
American Family Mutl Ins Co SI	Madison	6000 American Parkway	WI	53783	608-249-2111
American Standard Ins Co of WI	Madison	6000 American Parkway	WI	53783	608-249-2111
Geico General Ins Co	Chevy Chase	5260 Western Avenue	MD	20815	800-841-3000
USAA General Indemnity Co	San Antonio	9800 Fredericksburg Road	TX	78288	210-498-1411

Nevada

B+

Name	City	Address	State	Zip	Telephone
American Family Mutl Ins Co SI	Madison	6000 American Parkway	WI	53783	608-249-2111
American Standard Ins Co of WI	Madison	6000 American Parkway	WI	53783	608-249-2111
Geico General Ins Co	Chevy Chase	5260 Western Avenue	MD	20815	800-841-3000
USAA General Indemnity Co	San Antonio	9800 Fredericksburg Road	TX	78288	210-498-1411

New Hampshire

B+

Name	City	Address	State	Zip	Telephone
Geico General Ins Co	Chevy Chase	5260 Western Avenue	MD	20815	800-841-3000
Interins Exchange	Costa Mesa	3333 Fairview Road	CA	92626	714-850-5111
USAA General Indemnity Co	San Antonio	9800 Fredericksburg Road	TX	78288	210-498-1411

New Jersey

B+

Name	City	Address	State	Zip	Telephone
Progressive Garden State Ins Co	West Trenton	820 Bear Tavern Rd Suite 305	NJ	08628	440-461-5000
USAA General Indemnity Co	San Antonio	9800 Fredericksburg Road	TX	78288	210-498-1411

New Mexico

B+

Name	City	Address	State	Zip	Telephone
Geico General Ins Co	Chevy Chase	5260 Western Avenue	MD	20815	800-841-3000
Interins Exchange	Costa Mesa	3333 Fairview Road	CA	92626	714-850-5111
USAA General Indemnity Co	San Antonio	9800 Fredericksburg Road	TX	78288	210-498-1411

New York

B+

Name	City	Address	State	Zip	Telephone
Geico General Ins Co	Chevy Chase	5260 Western Avenue	MD	20815	800-841-3000
USAA General Indemnity Co	San Antonio	9800 Fredericksburg Road	TX	78288	210-498-1411

North Carolina

A-

Name	City	Address	State	Zip	Telephone
Cincinnati Indemnity Co	Fairfield	6200 South Gilmore Road	OH	45014	513-870-2000

B+

Name	City	Address	State	Zip	Telephone
USAA General Indemnity Co	San Antonio	9800 Fredericksburg Road	TX	78288	210-498-1411

North Dakota

B+

Name	City	Address	State	Zip	Telephone
American Family Mutl Ins Co SI	Madison	6000 American Parkway	WI	53783	608-249-2111
American Standard Ins Co of WI	Madison	6000 American Parkway	WI	53783	608-249-2111
Geico General Ins Co	Chevy Chase	5260 Western Avenue	MD	20815	800-841-3000
USAA General Indemnity Co	San Antonio	9800 Fredericksburg Road	TX	78288	210-498-1411

Ohio

B+

Name	City	Address	State	Zip	Telephone
American Family Mutl Ins Co SI	Madison	6000 American Parkway	WI	53783	608-249-2111
Geico General Ins Co	Chevy Chase	5260 Western Avenue	MD	20815	800-841-3000
USAA General Indemnity Co	San Antonio	9800 Fredericksburg Road	TX	78288	210-498-1411

Oklahoma

B+

Name	City	Address	State	Zip	Telephone
Geico General Ins Co	Chevy Chase	5260 Western Avenue	MD	20815	800-841-3000
USAA General Indemnity Co	San Antonio	9800 Fredericksburg Road	TX	78288	210-498-1411

Oregon

B+

Name	City	Address	State	Zip	Telephone
American Family Mutl Ins Co SI	Madison	6000 American Parkway	WI	53783	608-249-2111
American Standard Ins Co of WI	Madison	6000 American Parkway	WI	53783	608-249-2111
Geico General Ins Co	Chevy Chase	5260 Western Avenue	MD	20815	800-841-3000
USAA General Indemnity Co	San Antonio	9800 Fredericksburg Road	TX	78288	210-498-1411

Pennsylvania

B+

Name	City	Address	State	Zip	Telephone
Geico General Ins Co	Chevy Chase	5260 Western Avenue	MD	20815	800-841-3000
Interins Exchange	Costa Mesa	3333 Fairview Road	CA	92626	714-850-5111
USAA General Indemnity Co	San Antonio	9800 Fredericksburg Road	TX	78288	210-498-1411

Rhode Island

B+

Name	City	Address	State	Zip	Telephone
Geico General Ins Co	Chevy Chase	5260 Western Avenue	MD	20815	800-841-3000
USAA General Indemnity Co	San Antonio	9800 Fredericksburg Road	TX	78288	210-498-1411

South Carolina

B+

Name	City	Address	State	Zip	Telephone
American Family Mutl Ins Co SI	Madison	6000 American Parkway	WI	53783	608-249-2111
USAA General Indemnity Co	San Antonio	9800 Fredericksburg Road	TX	78288	210-498-1411

South Dakota

B+

Name	City	Address	State	Zip	Telephone
American Family Mutl Ins Co SI	Madison	6000 American Parkway	WI	53783	608-249-2111
American Standard Ins Co of WI	Madison	6000 American Parkway	WI	53783	608-249-2111
Geico General Ins Co	Chevy Chase	5260 Western Avenue	MD	20815	800-841-3000
USAA General Indemnity Co	San Antonio	9800 Fredericksburg Road	TX	78288	210-498-1411

Tennessee

B+

Name	City	Address	State	Zip	Telephone
Geico General Ins Co	Chevy Chase	5260 Western Avenue	MD	20815	800-841-3000
USAA General Indemnity Co	San Antonio	9800 Fredericksburg Road	TX	78288	210-498-1411

Texas

B+

Name	City	Address	State	Zip	Telephone
Geico General Ins Co	Chevy Chase	5260 Western Avenue	MD	20815	800-841-3000
USAA General Indemnity Co	San Antonio	9800 Fredericksburg Road	TX	78288	210-498-1411

Utah

B+

Name	City	Address	State	Zip	Telephone
American Family Mutl Ins Co SI	Madison	6000 American Parkway	WI	53783	608-249-2111
American Standard Ins Co of WI	Madison	6000 American Parkway	WI	53783	608-249-2111
Geico General Ins Co	Chevy Chase	5260 Western Avenue	MD	20815	800-841-3000
USAA General Indemnity Co	San Antonio	9800 Fredericksburg Road	TX	78288	210-498-1411

Vermont

B+

Name	City	Address	State	Zip	Telephone
Geico General Ins Co	Chevy Chase	5260 Western Avenue	MD	20815	800-841-3000
Interins Exchange	Costa Mesa	3333 Fairview Road	CA	92626	714-850-5111
USAA General Indemnity Co	San Antonio	9800 Fredericksburg Road	TX	78288	210-498-1411

Virginia

B+

Name	City	Address	State	Zip	Telephone
Alfa Alliance Ins Corp	Glen Allen	4480 Cox Road Suite 300	VA	23060	334-288-3900
Geico General Ins Co	Chevy Chase	5260 Western Avenue	MD	20815	800-841-3000
Interins Exchange	Costa Mesa	3333 Fairview Road	CA	92626	714-850-5111
USAA General Indemnity Co	San Antonio	9800 Fredericksburg Road	TX	78288	210-498-1411

Washington

B+

Name	City	Address	State	Zip	Telephone
American Family Mutl Ins Co SI	Madison	6000 American Parkway	WI	53783	608-249-2111
American Standard Ins Co of WI	Madison	6000 American Parkway	WI	53783	608-249-2111
Geico General Ins Co	Chevy Chase	5260 Western Avenue	MD	20815	800-841-3000
USAA General Indemnity Co	San Antonio	9800 Fredericksburg Road	TX	78288	210-498-1411

West Virginia

B+

Name	City	Address	State	Zip	Telephone
Geico General Ins Co	Chevy Chase	5260 Western Avenue	MD	20815	800-841-3000
USAA General Indemnity Co	San Antonio	9800 Fredericksburg Road	TX	78288	210-498-1411

Wisconsin

B+

Name	City	Address	State	Zip	Telephone
American Family Mutl Ins Co SI	Madison	6000 American Parkway	WI	53783	608-249-2111
American Standard Ins Co of WI	Madison	6000 American Parkway	WI	53783	608-249-2111
Geico General Ins Co	Chevy Chase	5260 Western Avenue	MD	20815	800-841-3000
USAA General Indemnity Co	San Antonio	9800 Fredericksburg Road	TX	78288	210-498-1411

Wyoming

B+

Name	City	Address	State	Zip	Telephone
Geico General Ins Co	Chevy Chase	5260 Western Avenue	MD	20815	800-841-3000
USAA General Indemnity Co	San Antonio	9800 Fredericksburg Road	TX	78288	210-498-1411

Appendices

Quote Comparison Worksheet for a Car Loan

	Creditor 1	Creditor 2	Creditor 3
Negotiated Price of Car	$	$	$
Down Payment	$	$	$
Trade-In Allowance (If trading in your car, this may involve negative equity)	$	$	$
Extended Service Contract (Optional)*	$	$	$
Credit Insurance (Optional)*	$	$	$
Guaranteed Auto Protection (Optional)*	$	$	$
Other Optional* Products	$	$	$
Amount Financed	$	$	$
Annual Percentage Rate (APR)	%	%	%
Finance Charge	$	$	$
Length of Contract in Months	$	$	$
Number of Payments	$	$	$
Monthly Payment Amount	$	$	$

* Note: You are not required to buy items that are optional. If you do not want these items, tell the dealer and do not sign for them. Be sure they are not included in the monthly payments or elsewhere on a contract that you sign.

Source: https://www.consumer.ftc.gov/articles/0056-financing-or-leasing-car#Get

Quote Comparison Worksheet for Auto Insurance

Using the worksheet below is a great way to stay organized as you compare the premium quotes from different insurance companies. It allows you to easily compare companies and how much they will charge you for each type of coverage you may be considering.

If you are planning to contact more than three companies, make copies of this worksheet beforehand.

Company Name						
Phone # or Web						
Address						
	Limit/Deductible	Price	Limit/Deductible	Price	Limit/Deductible	Price
Bodily Injury						
Property Damage						
Medical Payments /Personal Injury Payments						
Un/Under Insured Motorist						
Collision						
Comprehensive						
Roadside Assistance						
Rental Car Reimbursement						
Loan/Lease Payoff						
Other						
Discounts						
TOTAL						

Helpful Resources

Contact any of the following organizations for further information about purchasing auto insurance.

- **Your state department of insurance** - See next page for a specific contact
- **National Association of Insurance Commissioners** - www.naic.org
- **Insurance Information Institute** - www.iii.org
- **Independent Insurance Agents & Brokers of America**
  www.independentagent.com/default.aspx
- **Weiss Ratings, LLC**. - www.weissratings.com

The following is a partial listing of websites that give auto insurance quotes

Weiss Ratings does not endorse any of these companies, nor do we warranty any of the information you may obtain from these sites. This information is being provided strictly for your reference only to show the vast number of sites available when shopping for auto insurance.

Company websites

www.21st.com
www.AARP.TheHartford.com
www.Allstate.com
www.ElectricInsurance.com
www.Esurance.com
www.Geico.com
www.USAA.com

www.LibertyMutual.com
www.nationalgeneral.com
www.Nationwide.com
www.Progressive.com
www.StateAuto.com
www.StateFarm.com

Independent websites

www.AutoInsuranceGroup.com
www.ComparisonMarket.com
www.Insurance.com

www.Insure.com
www.trustedchoice.com

State Insurance Commissioners'
Departmental Contact Information

State	Official's Title	Website Address	Telephone
Alabama	Commissioner	www.aldoi.org	(334) 269-3550
Alaska	Director	https://www.commerce.alaska.gov/web/ins/	(800) 467-8725
Arizona	Director	https://insurance.az.gov/	(602) 364-2499
Arkansas	Commissioner	www.insurance.arkansas.gov	(800) 852-5494
California	Commissioner	www.insurance.ca.gov	(800) 927-4357
Colorado	Commissioner	https://www.colorado.gov/pacific/dora/node/90616	(800) 866-7675
Connecticut	Commissioner	http://www.ct.gov/cid/site/default.asp	(800) 203-3447
Delaware	Commissioner	http://delawareinsurance.gov/	(800) 282-8611
Dist. of Columbia	Commissioner	http://disb.dc.gov/	(202) 727-8000
Florida	Commissioner	www.floir.com/	(850) 413-3140
Georgia	Commissioner	www.oci.ga.gov/	(800) 656-2298
Hawaii	Commissioner	http://cca.hawaii.gov/ins/	(808) 586-2790
Idaho	Director	www.doi.idaho.gov	(800) 721-3272
Illinois	Director	www.insurance.illinois.gov/	(866) 445-5364
Indiana	Commissioner	www.in.gov/idoi/	(800) 622-4461
Iowa	Commissioner	https://iid.iowa.gov/	(877) 955-1212
Kansas	Commissioner	www.ksinsurance.org	(800) 432-2484
Kentucky	Commissioner	http://insurance.ky.gov/	(800) 595-6053
Louisiana	Commissioner	www.ldi.la.gov/	(800) 259-5300
Maine	Superintendent	www.maine.gov/pfr/insurance/	(800) 300-5000
Maryland	Commissioner	http://insurance.maryland.gov/Pages/default.aspx	(800) 492-6116
Massachusetts	Commissioner	www.mass.gov/ocabr/government/oca-agencies/doi-lp/	(877) 563-4467
Michigan	Director	http://www.michigan.gov/difs	(877) 999-6442
Minnesota	Commissioner	http://mn.gov/commerce/	(651) 539-1500
Mississippi	Commissioner	http://www.mid.ms.gov/	(601) 359-3569
Missouri	Director	www.insurance.mo.gov	(800) 726-7390
Montana	Commissioner	http://csimt.gov/	(800) 332-6148
Nebraska	Director	www.doi.nebraska.gov/	(402) 471-2201
Nevada	Commissioner	www.doi.nv.gov/	(888) 872-3234
New Hampshire	Commissioner	www.nh.gov/insurance/	(800) 852-3416
New Jersey	Commissioner	www.state.nj.us/dobi/	(800) 446-7467
New Mexico	Superintendent	www.osi.state.nm.us/	(855) 427-5674
New York	Superintendent	www.dfs.ny.gov/	(800) 342-3736
North Carolina	Commissioner	www.ncdoi.com	(855) 408-1212
North Dakota	Commissioner	www.nd.gov/ndins/	(800) 247-0560
Ohio	Lieutenant Governor	www.insurance.ohio.gov	(800) 686-1526
Oklahoma	Commissioner	www.ok.gov/oid/	(800) 522-0071
Oregon Insurance	Commissioner	http://dfr.oregon.gov/Pages/index.aspx	(888) 877-4894
Pennsylvania	Commissioner	www.insurance.pa.gov/	(877) 881-6388
Puerto Rico	Commissioner	www.ocs.gobierno.pr	(787) 304-8686
Rhode Island	Superintendent	www.dbr.state.ri.us/divisions/insurance/	(401) 462-9500
South Carolina	Director	www.doi.sc.gov	(803) 737-6160
South Dakota	Director	http://dlr.sd.gov/insurance/default.aspx	(605) 773-3563
Tennessee	Commissioner	http://tn.gov/commerce/	(615) 741-2241
Texas	Commissioner	www.tdi.texas.gov/	(800) 578-4677
Utah	Commissioner	www.insurance.utah.gov	(800) 439-3805
Vermont	Commissioner	www.dfr.vermont.gov/	(802) 828-3301
Virgin Islands	Lieutenant Governor	http://ltg.gov.vi/division-of-banking-and-insurance.html	(340) 774-7166
Virginia	Commissioner	www.scc.virginia.gov/boi/	(804) 371-9741
Washington	Commissioner	www.insurance.wa.gov	(800) 562-6900
West Virginia	Commissioner	www.wvinsurance.gov	(888) 879-9842
Wisconsin	Commissioner	oci.wi.gov	(800) 236-8517
Wyoming	Commissioner	http://doi.wyo.gov/	(800) 438-5768

Glossary

This glossary contains the most important terms used in this publication.

Agent	An insurance professional that sells insurance for one or more insurance companies. Exclusive agents sell for one company while independent agents sell for more than one company.
Assigned Risk Plan	A state supervised program that assigns a person to a company for insurance because that person cannot get auto insurance from a regular carrier.
Book Value	The value of your vehicle as determined by your insurance company.
Claim	A request to your insurance company to pay for your loss or damage you caused that is covered under your insurance policy. First-party claims are your claims to your company, and third-party claims are your claims against another person's insurance company.
Collision Coverage	Optional insurance that pays for damage to your car caused by a collision with another car or object.
Comprehensive Coverage	Optional insurance which pays for damage to your vehicle caused by items other than collision such as vandalism, theft, fire, or hail among other items.
Deductible	The amount you will pay out of pocket when you file an insurance claim, before your insurance company will start to pay you.
Exclusion	A type of loss that your policy will not cover.
First-party Claims	Your claims made to your own insurance company as opposed to third-party claims that you make to another person's insurance company.

Gap Coverage	An extra coverage that can be purchased to cover the difference between the amount you owe on your vehicle and the amount the insurance company will pay you. This coverage is usually for leased vehicles but can also be purchased for vehicles that are financed.
Insurance Department	A state agency that monitors insurance company activities in that state. It also assists consumers with insurance issues such as complaints and education.
Liability	A legally enforceable financial obligation.
Liability Coverage	Insurance which pays for the losses of other people which you cause accidentally or negligently. Bodily injury liability pays for medical costs of others and your legal costs if a suit is brought. Property damage liability pays for damage you cause to some else's car or property.
Medical Payments Coverage	Optional insurance in states without "no-fault" insurance. This coverage pays for medical expenses and funeral expenses for you and your passengers regardless of who is at fault.
Negligence	Failure to exercise a generally acceptable level of care and caution.
No-fault Insurance	Insurance under which each driver seeks payment from his or her own insurance company regardless of fault.
Personal Injury Protection (PIP)	A broader form of medical payments insurance coverage that offers protection for expenses incurred up to a specific, per-person dollar amount. Mandatory coverage in states with no-fault statutes, and optional in states without no-fault coverage.
Policy Period	The length of time an insurance policy is valid.
Premium	The amount of money you pay for coverage.

Subrogation

The act of an insurance company seeking reimbursement from another insurance company for an amount they paid to their own policyholder for an accident in which the other company's policyholder was at fault.

Under- or Uninsured Motorist Coverage

Insurance which pays for accidents caused by someone who has insufficient coverage or no coverage at all. This includes hit-and-run drivers.

SOURCES

Part 1:

https://blog.nationwide.com/how-to-test-drive-a-car/

https://www.bankofamerica.com/auto-loans/how-car-loans-work/

https://www.consumer.ftc.gov/articles/0056-financing-or-leasing-car#Get

https://www.consumerreports.org/buying-a-car/how-to-find-the-right-car-for-you/

https://www.edmunds.com/car-buying/how-to-review-your-new-car-sales-contract.html

https://www.edmunds.com/car-buying/how-to-test-drive-a-car.html

https://www.insure.com/car-insurance/insurance-rates-by-car.html

https://www.magnifymoney.com/blog/auto-loan/11-things-know-lease-car/

https://www.nerdwallet.com/blog/loans/auto-loans/buy-used-car/

https://www.npr.org/2017/05/09/527574528/buying-a-car-what-to-look-for-when-you-take-a-test-drive

https://www.thesimpledollar.com/the-big-debate-2-leasing-buying-new-or-buying-used/

https://www.valuepenguin.com/auto-insurance/buy-used-car-private-seller

Part 2 of this guide is derived from *Weiss Ratings' Consumer Guide to Auto Insurance*, Spring 2020 edition.

Weiss Ratings: What Our Ratings Mean

A **Excellent.** The company offers excellent financial security. It has maintained a conservative stance in its investment strategies, business operations and underwriting commitments. While the financial position of any company is subject to change, we believe that this company has the resources necessary to deal with severe economic conditions.

B **Good.** The company offers good financial security and has the resources to deal with a variety of adverse economic conditions. It comfortably exceeds the minimum levels for all of our rating criteria, and is likely to remain healthy for the near future. However, in the event of a severe recession or major financial crisis, we feel that this assessment should be reviewed to make sure that the firm is still maintaining adequate financial strength.

C **Fair.** The company offers fair financial security and is currently stable. But during an economic downturn or other financial pressures, we feel it may encounter difficulties in maintaining its financial stability.

D **Weak.** The company currently demonstrates what, in our opinion, we consider to be significant weaknesses which could negatively impact policyholders. In an unfavorable economic environment, these weaknesses could be magnified.

E **Very Weak.** The company currently demonstrates what we consider to be significant weaknesses and has also failed some of the basic tests that we use to identify fiscal stability. Therefore, even in a favorable economic environment, it is our opinion that policyholders could incur significant risks.

F **Failed.** The company is deemed failed if it is either 1) under supervision of an insurance regulatory authority; 2) in the process of rehabilitation; 3) in the process of liquidation; or 4) voluntarily dissolve after disciplinary or other regulatory action by an insurance regulatory authority.

+ The plus sign is an indication that the company is in the upper third of the letter grade.
- The minus sign is an indication that the company is in the lower third of the letter grade.
U Unrated. The company is unrated for one or more of the following reasons: (1) total assets are less than $1 million; (2) premium income for the current year was less than $100,000; or (3) the company functions almost exclusively as a holding company rather than as an underwriter; or, (4) in our opinion, we do not have enough information to reliably issue a rating.

Terms and Conditions

This document is prepared strictly for the confidential use of our customer(s). It has been provided to you at your specific request. It is not directed to, or intended for distribution to or use by, any person or entity who is a citizen or resident of or located in any locality, state, country or other jurisdiction where such distribution, publication, availability or use would be contrary to law or regulation or which would subject Weiss Ratings, LLC or its affiliates to any registration or licensing requirement within such jurisdiction.

No part of the analysts' compensation was, is, or will be, directly or indirectly, related to the specific recommendations or views expressed in this research report.

This document is not intended for the direct or indirect solicitation of business. Weiss Ratings, LLC, and its affiliates disclaim any and all liability to any person or entity for any loss or damage caused, in whole or in part, by any error (negligent or otherwise) or other circumstances involved in, resulting from or relating to the procurement, compilation, analysis, interpretation, editing, transcribing, publishing and/or dissemination or transmittal of any information contained herein.

Weiss Ratings, LLC has not taken any steps to ensure that the securities or investment vehicle referred to in this report are suitable for any particular investor. The investment or services contained or referred to in this report may not be suitable for you and it is recommended that you consult an independent investment advisor if you are in doubt about such investments or investment services. Nothing in this report constitutes investment, legal, accounting or tax advice or a representation that any investment or strategy is suitable or appropriate to your individual circumstances or otherwise constitutes a personal recommendation to you.

The ratings and other opinions contained in this document must be construed solely as statements of opinion from Weiss Ratings, LLC, and not statements of fact. Each rating or opinion must be weighed solely as a factor in your choice of an institution and should not be construed as a recommendation to buy, sell or otherwise act with respect to the particular product or company involved.

Past performance should not be taken as an indication or guarantee of future performance, and no representation or warranty, expressed or implied, is made regarding future performance. Information, opinions and estimates contained in this report reflect a judgment at its original date of publication and are subject to change without notice. Weiss Ratings, LLC offers a notification service for rating changes on companies you specify. For more information visit WeissRatings.com or call 1-877-934-7778. The price, value and income from any of the securities or financial instruments mentioned in this report can fall as well as rise.

This document and the information contained herein is copyrighted by Weiss Ratings, LLC. Any copying, displaying, selling, distributing or otherwise delivering of this information or any part of this document to any other person or entity is prohibited without the express written consent of Weiss Ratings, LLC, with the exception of a reviewer or editor who may quote brief passages in connection with a review or a news story.

Weiss Ratings' Mission Statement
Weiss Ratings' mission is to empower consumers, professionals, and institutions with high quality advisory information for selecting or monitoring a financial services company or financial investment. In doing so, Weiss Ratings will adhere to the highest ethical standards by maintaining our independent, unbiased outlook and approach to advising our customers.

https://greyhouse.weissratings.com

Financial Ratings Series, published by Weiss Ratings and Grey House Publishing offers libraries, schools, universities and the business community a wide range of investing, banking, insurance and financial literacy tools. Visit www.greyhouse.com or https://greyhouse.weissratings.com for more information about the titles and online tools below.

- Weiss Ratings Financial Literacy Basics
- Weiss Ratings Financial Literacy: Planning For the Future
- Weiss Ratings Financial Literacy: How to Become an Investor
- Weiss Ratings Guide to Banks
- Weiss Ratings Guide to Credit Unions
- Weiss Ratings Guide to Health Insurers
- Weiss Ratings Guide to Property & Casualty Insurers
- Weiss Ratings Guide to Life & Annuity Insurers
- Weiss Ratings Investment Research Guide to Stocks
- Weiss Ratings Investment Research Guide to Bond & Money Market Mutual Funds
- Weiss Ratings Investment Research Guide to Stock Mutual Funds
- Weiss Ratings Investment Research Guide to Exchange-Traded Funds
- Weiss Ratings Consumer Guides
- Weiss Ratings Medicare Supplement Insurance Buyers Guide
- Financial Ratings Series Online – **https://greyhouse.weissratings.com**